# The God of glory
## Ezekiel

Series Editor: Tim Chester

The God of glory
Ezekiel: a good book guide
© Tim Chester/The Good Book Company, 2005. Reprinted 2010.

The Good Book Company
The Good Book Company
Tel: 0333 123 0880
International:+44 (0) 208 942 0880
Email: admin@thegoodbook.co.uk
Websites
UK: www.thegoodbook.co.uk
N America: www.thegoodbook.com
Australia: www.thegoodbook.com.au
New Zealand: www.thegoodbook.co.nz

ISBN 9781904889274

Printed in China

# CONTENTS

# Introduction: Good Book Guides

Every Bible-study group is different—yours may take place in a church building, in a home, in a cafe, on a train, over a leisurely mid-morning coffee or squashed into a 30-minute lunch break. Your group may include new Christians, mature Christians, non-Christians, mums and tots, students, businessmen or teens. That's why we've designed these Good Book Guides to be flexible for use in many different situations.

Our aim in each session is to uncover the meaning of a passage, and see how it fits into the "big picture" of the Bible. But that can never be the end. We also need to appropriately apply what we have discovered to our lives. Let's take a look at what is included:

⊕ **Talkabout:** Most groups need to "break the ice" at the beginning of a session, and here's the question that will do that. It's designed to get people talking around a subject that will be covered in the course of the Bible study.

⬇ **Investigate:** The Bible text for each session is broken up into manageable chunks, with questions that aim to help you understand what the passage is about. The **Leader's Guide** contains **guidance on questions**, and sometimes ⊠ additional "follow-up" questions.

⊡ **Explore more (optional):** These questions will help you connect what you have learned to other parts of the Bible, so you can begin to understand how the Bible fits together as a whole.

➔ **Apply:** As you go through a Bible study, you'll keep coming across **apply** sections. These are questions to get the group discussing what the Bible teaching means in practice for you and your church.

⊡ **Getting personal** is an opportunity for you to think, plan and pray about the changes that you personally may need to make as a result of what you have learned.

⬆ **Pray:** We want to encourage prayer that is rooted in God's word—in line with His concerns, purposes and promises. So each session ends with an opportunity to review the truths and challenges highlighted by the Bible study, and turn them into prayers of request and thanksgiving.

The **Leader's Guide** provides historical background information, explanations of the Bible texts for each session, ideas for **optional extra** activities, and guidance on how best to help people uncover the truths of God's word.

# Why study Ezekiel?

*Do not be afraid of what they say or terrified by them, though they are a rebellious house. You must speak my words to them, whether they listen or fail to listen, for they are rebellious.*

*But you, son of man, listen to what I say to you. Do not rebel like that rebellious house; open your mouth and eat what I give you.*
**Ezekiel 2 v 6-8**

Few books of the Bible seem scarier than Ezekiel—48 chapters of weird and wonderful visions, bizarre street performances and blood-curdling judgments. Perhaps you've wondered what it's all about. But will you ever have the time to study such a large book? And does this stuff really have anything to say to you?

This Bible-study course will take you through the whole of Ezekiel in just six sessions! This whistle-stop tour gives a clear overview of all the main themes of Ezekiel's prophecy—God's glory, judgment, and hope—focusing on key passages that explain the surrounding chapters.

But more than that, you'll discover how God's word to His exiled people is truly fulfilled in the gospel of Jesus and the experience of Christians.

"Then they will know that I am the LORD" is the repeated message of Ezekiel. In a world of false hopes that will ultimately fail, this is a message for everyone.

# 1

## Ezekiel 1 – 3
# THE GOD OF GLORY

## ⊕ talkabout

**1.** What discourages you about the state of the church today? What gives you cause for hope?

## ⊥ investigate

At the beginning of the book of Ezekiel, the last remaining part of the nation of Israel (the southern kingdom of Judah) has been smashed by the Babylonians, the top nation of the day. The ruling class and all the promising young men have all been taken off into exile in Babylon. A puppet regime has been set up in Jerusalem, under Babylonian control. Ezekiel was among those carried off into exile.

**2.** How do you think the exiles would have felt in Babylon?

**3.** What doubts about God would the exiles have had?

**▶ Read Ezekiel 1 v 1-28**

**4.** Why is it significant that Ezekiel sees this vision of God in Babylon?

**5.** What details of Ezekiel's vision show the power and glory of God?

**6.** Why is it significant that God is on a throne with wheels?

**7.** How does Ezekiel respond to this vision?

In verse 28, Ezekiel says that what he saw was "the appearance of the likeness of the glory of the LORD". He did not even see the real thing—only something that *looked like* God's glory! Ezekiel refers back to this vision on a number of occasions (see 3 v 12-15, 23; 10 v 15-22; 43 v 3). The book of Ezekiel has a phrase that is repeated more than 60 times: **"Then they will know that I am the LORD".** God is at the centre of Ezekiel's message and at the centre of Ezekiel's view of the world.

## ⊟ **apply**

**8.** In what ways might our prayers, our evangelism, and our meetings be too human-centred? Think of one concrete change for each of these that would make them more God-centred.

 The God of glory

• Why do you think we keep moving away from "God-centredness"?

• What effect does human-centred "Christianity" have on people?

## ⊡ getting personal

What impression of God would someone pick up from watching the way in which you live out your Christian faith? Would that impression be anything like Ezekiel's vision?

## ⊡ explore more

Look at verses 26-28. At the heart of Ezekiel's vision is "a figure like that of a man". What is the significance of this? For a clue, look at the parallels with **Revelation 1 v 12-18**. How do we see the glory of God? See **John 1 v 14**.

## ⊻ investigate

**▶ Read Ezekiel 2 v 1 – 3 v 15**

**9.** How will the people respond to Ezekiel's message?

**10.** According to 3 v 6-7, what is the reason why people reject God's word?

📖 **explore more**

Look at **Psalm 14 v 1**. Why does the fool say there is no God?

Look at **Romans 1 v 18-25**. Why do people not know God?

How do these references explain why Ezekiel's message will be rejected?

**11.** How will Ezekiel cope with the rejection and opposition of people to his message?

## ➔ apply

**12.** People do not reject God's word because it is too hard to understand, but because they do not want to obey it. What does this mean for our evangelism?

**13.** When people accept the message about Jesus, how much is their positive response due to our abilities to reason with and persuade them? See 1 Corinthians 2 v 1-5.

• What part do Christians play in evangelism? See 2 Corinthians 4 v 1-6.

**14.** What encouragements are there in these chapters when we are discouraged by the state of church and society today?

## ⊡ getting personal

• What do you truly think about evangelism? That it's pointless in today's cynical, pleasure-seeking society, with its philosophy of "believe whatever's right for you"? That it's a great thing for gifted Christians to do, but as you're not one of them you needn't get involved? How should the message of Ezekiel's vision and calling change you?

## ⊡ pray

**Thank God...**
• that He is still the same God that Ezekiel saw in his vision.
• that we too have seen the glory of God—His grace and His truth, in Jesus.
• that despite the rebellion of humanity and the weakness of His people, God has, and always will, preserve His people and His gospel.

**Ask God...**
• to give you a vision of His glory in Jesus Christ...

... that will keep you going when people reject His word.

... that will enable you to live a God-centred life, becoming a demonstration of the Spirit's power to those around you.

• to give this vision of Jesus to His suffering and persecuted people throughout the world.

# 2 Ezekiel 4 – 24
# THE GOD OF JUDGMENT

## ⊕ talkabout

**1.** What kind of things do people hope for the future?

## ⊕ investigate

> **Read Ezekiel 4 v 1-3 and 5 v 1-13**

**2.** Why did Ezekiel get a haircut? What did it mean?

**3.** What was Jerusalem's relationship to the nations supposed to be (5 v 5)? See Deuteronomy 4 v 5-8.

**4.** What was Jerusalem's relationship to the nations in reality?

**5.** God set Jerusalem in the centre of the nations (5 v 5) to be a light to them. Discuss where God has placed your group and the individuals within it. What opportunities do you have to be a light to those around you?

- How should Christians go about being a light to people like this (see, for example Titus 2 v 1-10)?

- Think of examples of what it means to *go beyond* the standards of those around us.

- What should be the effect of this way of life (see Titus 2 v 5, 8 and 10)?

⊡ **getting personal**

What reaction to the gospel could your way of life provoke in those around you? Understanding of God's wisdom and righteousness, or rejection and slander of the gospel? Think about all the areas of your life where you meet non-Christians. Are you failing even to live up to the standards of those around you?

## ⬇ investigate

In chapter 10 Ezekiel sees the glory of God leave the temple (see especially verses 18-19). God is no longer with His people. He is no longer for them. But in 5 v 8 Ezekiel describes something even worse —God is *against* His people.

**❯ Read Ezekiel 12 v 21 – 13 v 12**

**6.** What hopes did the people have? How were these hopes strengthened (see 13 v 10)?

**7.** What was Ezekiel's response to their hopes?

## ⊡ explore more

**Read Ezekiel 18 v 1-4 and 19-32**

What is the people's complaint? What is God's response? If God judges a person according to their actions, what hope is there for any of us? What evidence for verse 32 can be found in God's word?

**❯ Read Ezekiel 24 v 15-27**

**8.** Who was the delight of Ezekiel's eyes, and what was the delight of the people of Israel? Were these good things to delight in?

**9.** What would God do about the things His people loved?

• What is shocking about God's response (see v 21) and what was the reason for it?

**10.** What effect would God's action have on the people (see v 23)? And what would be the final outcome (v 24)?

## ➔ apply

**11.** Ezekiel destroys the false hopes of the people. What are the popular false hopes that Christians need to knock down today? Try to come up with one for each area:
• religion
• consumerism
• humanism
• in our churches

• How can we identify today's false prophets (see 2 Timothy 4 v 1-5)?

• How should Christians go about destroying these false hopes?

The God of glory

**12.** How has this study of Ezekiel's message changed your view of God?

- In what way have we learned that "God will be God"?

- What does this mean for us as Christians, the present-day people of God (see 2 Corinthians 11 v 2-4)?

- Where can hope be found?

### ⊡ pray

From the passage write down three things to thank and praise God for, and three things to ask for.

**Thank God...**


**Ask God...**

# 3 Ezekiel 25 – 32
# THE GOD OF THE NATIONS

## ⊕ talkabout

1. What contacts do you have with those of other faiths and cultures? How do you feel about telling them the Christian message?

## ⊕ investigate

> **Read Ezekiel 25**

2. What were the sins of the nations around Israel?

> **Read Ezekiel 28 v 11-19 and 24**

3. What were the sins of Tyre?

## ⊞ explore more

optional

Compare what Ezekiel says about Tyre with **Revelation 18**. What is John's message to the Christians under Roman rule (Rome is depicted as Babylon)? See 18 v 4. What is the message to us?

**▶ Read Ezekiel 29 v 1-7**

**4.** Why is Egypt singled out for special treatment (see also verse 16)?

## ⊕ apply

**5.** Look at 29 v 16. To what or whom might we turn to for help as a substitute for trust in God...

- for our own personal security (see Matthew 6 v 19-21)?

- for a solution to the problems of our society or threats to our way of life (see Isaiah 31 v 1)?

- for a solution to the weakness and insignificance of the church (see 1 Corinthians 1 v 20-25)?

- What was the result for Israel of trusting in Egypt? For us, what is the result of trusting in substitutes for God?

## ⊙ investigate

Israel had been defeated by the Babylonians. Some of the nations were saying, "Great! This is our opportunity" (25 v 6). But the nations should not delight in Israel's downfall. Others were saying: "Israel's God is no better than our gods" (25 v 8). But the nations should not misunderstand Israel's downfall.

**6.** Look at 5 v 8. What was Ezekiel's message to Israel?

**7.** Look at 26 v 3. What was Ezekiel's message to the nations?

**8.** Look at 6 v 10, 13-14. What was Ezekiel's message to Israel?

**9.** Look at 25 v 7, 11, 17. What was Ezekiel's message to the nations?

**10.** What should people from other nations think about Israel's defeat?

**11.** What should people from other nations think about Israel's God?

We might be tempted to think that Ezekiel's message to Israel has little to do with us, concluding that it is just a particular word to a particular people at a particular time. But chapters 25 – 32 show that God's judgment against Israel is a picture of His judgment against all humanity.

• Israel's God is the God of all humanity—God says to the nations what He said to Israel: "You will know that I am the Lord".

- Israel's fate is the fate of all humanity—God says to the nations what He said to Israel: "I am against you".

## ⊡ apply

**12.** Ezekiel shows that God is the God of all nations.
What happens to people when they believe that the God of the Bible is only the God of Israel, or of Christians?

- How might these chapters help us respond to someone who believes that all religions lead to God?

- How should the truth that God is the God of all nations affect... our prayers, our evangelism, our meetings, our friendships, and our involvement in international mission?

## ⊡ getting personal

How could you be more involved in bringing God's word to the nations?

How do you score in your knowledge of Christian brothers and sisters in other countries, your prayer for gospel work abroad, and your support of gospel workers far from home?

Are there any internationals in your community to whom you could reach out?

# ⊡ pray

**Thank God...**
- for opening your eyes to know that He is the Lord.
- that He has spoken His word—not only of judgment, but also of salvation—to all the nations, including you.
- that He is never a "splintered staff", but His faithfulness endures forever.

**Ask God...**
- to help you live a life that shows He is the Lord.
- to help Christians, churches and missionaries that you know in other countries, as they bring God's word to the nations.
- to show you how to be involved in bringing His word to the nations.

Ezekiel 33 – 36

# THE GOD OF HOPE

## ⊕ talkabout

1. Have you ever wished you could have a fresh start at something?

## ⊥ investigate

### ▶ Read Ezekiel 33 v 21-29

Chapters 4 – 24 have destroyed the false hope of Israel. Their capital city, Jerusalem, will be destroyed. Now the news comes: Jerusalem has indeed fallen. Now Ezekiel can speak of true hope—hope in God and His promises. Except that the people still cling to false hope.

2. Why are they still hopeful? But why are these false hopes?

## ⊡ explore more

### Read Ezekiel 33 v 30-33

In verse 30 it looks as if the people have a right attitude to God's word. But what is the reality? Why do the people like listening to Ezekiel? What makes a talk or Bible study worth listening to? How important is it that a talk is entertaining?

**>** **Read Ezekiel 34 v 1-10**

**3.** What is God's complaint against the leaders of Israel?

**>** **Read Ezekiel 34 v 11-29**

**4.** What will be God's response?

**5.** How will God shepherd His people?

### ⊡ explore more

optional

Compare verse 34 v 11 and 23. Will God Himself rescue His people or will God's King do it?

How is this solved by the identity of the good shepherd in **John 10 v 11-16 and 27-28**? What further information do these verses give us about how God will shepherd His people?

### ⊡ apply

**6.** What does it mean to live under the care of Jesus, as our Shepherd-King? (See Psalm 23.)

- See 1 Peter 5 v 1-4. How does Peter use the example of Jesus our Shepherd to teach leaders in the church?

- How should we respond to Jesus' powerful and sacrificial care of us?

## ⊡ getting personal

How difficult do you find it to have trust and confidence in Jesus to protect you and provide for all your needs? Why do we struggle in this area? What would help you to respond rightly to His powerful sacrificial care?

## ⊥ investigate

**❯ Read Ezekiel 34 v 25-31**

**7.** How does Ezekiel describe the reign of God's coming King?

Way back, God had promised Abraham (the father of Israel) a new people in a new land. Ezekiel has said that God Himself will gather His people and care for them. Now He promises to restore the land for them. In 36 v 35 Ezekiel describes it as a new Eden (the garden where Adam and Eve first lived).

The nation of Edom (Israel's neighbour) thought they could take advantage of Israel's defeat and seize the land (35 v 12). So Ezekiel compares the mountains of Edom (Mount Seir) and the mountains of Israel. God is against Mount Seir (35 v 2-4), but the mountains of Israel will be repopulated by God's people (36 v 8-12).

## ⊡ explore more

**Read Hebrews 11 v 8-16 and 39-40.** What does this tell us about God's promise of a land for Abraham's descendants? How was it understood by the faithful descendants of Abraham? **Read Romans 8 v 19-21 and Revelation 21 v 1.** How will God's promise to restore the land ultimately be fulfilled? **Read Matthew 5 v 5** to see who will benefit from that fulfilment.

> **Read Ezekiel 36 v 16-23**

**8.** Why will God save His people?

**9.** How was God's name honoured by Israel's judgment?

**10.** How will God's name be honoured by Israel's salvation?

**11.** Similarly, how does God glorify His name today?

> **Read Ezekiel 36 v 24-32**

**12.** God is going to give His people a fresh start, but much more than a fresh start. How will He do this?

# ⊟ apply

13. Now that this promise has been fulfilled in the gospel of Jesus, what changes should we expect to see in the life of someone who claims to have become a Christian? Eg: What new attitude to sin (see 1 John 1 v 8-9); what new attitude to God's word (see John 10 v 27)?

- What should our attitude be to those who claim to be Christians but show no evidence of these changes?

## ⊡ getting personal

If you are a Christian, how has Ezekiel 36 v 26-27 been fulfilled in your life? Do you only focus on the unfinished work and get down-hearted? Or can you thank God for how He has already changed you?

## ⬆ pray

**Thank God...**
- that Jesus is God's promised Shepherd-King, utterly able to protect us from all enemies and provide everything we need.
- for the "better heavenly land" that we will one day enter through Jesus.
- that the promise of a new, clean heart and spirit has finally been fulfilled in the gospel of Jesus, and is available to you.

**Ask God...**
- to help you put total trust and confidence in Jesus.
- to use you to help the helpless, harassed crowds of people in this world, who don't know Jesus as their Shepherd-King.
- to glorify His name in the message of judgment and salvation that comes through Christians preaching the gospel.

# 5 Ezekiel 37 – 39
# THE GOD OF LIFE

## ⊕ talkabout

1.  Have you ever been in a situation that you thought was hopeless?

## ⬇ investigate

> **Read Ezekiel 37 v 1-14**

2.  What do the dry bones represent?

In verse 11 the people say: "Our hope is gone" and the message of Ezekiel 4 – 24 was that the hopes of the people were false. Where do you find hope when hope is gone? The answer is in God.

3.  How does God bring new life to His people?

## ⤏ apply

**4.** What are the lessons that we can learn, for ourselves and our churches, from the story of the dry bones?

- God gives His people new life through His Word and His Spirit working together. What should this say to Christians or churches who emphasise only one of these two things? Is it a question of getting the right balance between two extremes? **See Ephesians 6 v 17.**

- What is your reaction to this story? Can you imagine the sight and sound of it? How should we respond to God, right now and in our daily lives?

## ⊡ getting personal

Do you have a story of new life from God? What difference does a change like this make to the way you think about...

- your pre-Christian life?
- non-Christians around you?
- gospel ministry?
- your prayers?

## ⊌ investigate

King Rehoboam, the son of Israel's most prosperous king, Solomon, ruled over the people of Israel harshly. As a result they rebelled against him. In 930 BC the kingdom of Israel split into two. The northern tribes formed a new nation under the leadership of Jeroboam. This nation took the name Israel, but it was also called Ephraim. Two hundred years later in 722 BC, it was defeated by the Assyrians and most of the people were taken away into exile. The southern kingdom, known as Judah, continued until 587 BC. Finally, they were defeated by the Babylonians and some of them—including Ezekiel—were exiled in Babylon.

**❯ Read Ezekiel 37 v 15-28**

5. What does Ezekiel's trick with the stick mean?

6. How does Ezekiel describe the reign of God's coming King?

## ⊡ explore more

The promise "They will be my people, and I will be their God" (v 23 and 27) occurs throughout the Bible. **Read Exodus 6 v 7.** How is this promised fulfilled in the church (see **2 Corinthians 6 v 16**)? How will it be fulfilled in the new creation (see **Revelation 21 v 3**)?

7. Ezekiel promised a united Israel, but in the New Testament, the apostle Paul says God had an even bigger plan in mind. See Ephesians 3 v 4-6, 10 and 4 v 1-3. What is that plan and what does it mean for us?

**❯ Read Ezekiel 38 v 1-23**

8. What is the threat facing God's people?

**9.** What hope for God's people is mentioned in these verses? See also 39 v 21-29.

**10.** What is God's purpose in allowing the threat and then destroying it?

Gog and Magog were not around at the time when Ezekiel was writing. These, and other names mentioned in these verses, come from Israel's ancient history (see Genesis 10 v 1-3). Ezekiel uses them symbolically. They represent all those throughout history who have opposed God and His people. The apostle John also uses the symbolism of Gog and Magog to suggest that this rebellion against God will come to a climax at the end of history (see Revelation 20 v 7-10). But God will defend His people. Ezekiel 39 describes God's total victory over those who oppose Him.

## ⤷ apply

**11.** How are God's people similarly threatened today?

• Why is it that God seemingly fails to rescue His people right now from these threats?

• How can these experiences make us stronger?

• What truth will help God's people to stand firm in these times?

⊡ **pray**

**Thank God...**
• for His Spirit and His word, that create such miraculous new life.
• that one day all God's creation will know that He is the Lord.
• (Think of your own reason for thanksgiving from Ezekiel 37 – 39.)

**Ask God...**
• to help persecuted Christians around the world have confidence in the
  hope of Ezekiel 39 v 25-29.
• to encourage those within the group facing pressure not to follow
  Christ.
• (Think of your own request for help that has come out of this session.)

# 6 Ezekiel 40 – 48
## THE GOD OF THE FUTURE

### ⊕ talkabout

1. What do you imagine heaven will be like?

### ⊥ investigate

> **Read Ezekiel 40 v 1-9**

2. How does Ezekiel picture God's promised future?

The temple was the symbol of God's presence with His people. But in chapter 33 Ezekiel learns that the city and temple have been destroyed by the Babylonians (33 v 21). God has abandoned His people because of their sin.

> **Read Ezekiel 43 v 1-12**

3. Compare these verses with Ezekiel 8 v 1-5 and 10 v 18-22. What are the similarities?

**4.** What is the great difference?

**5.** What behaviour does God expect in response to this vision of a new temple?

In chapters 8 – 10 Ezekiel sees the corrupt, idolatrous worship of the temple in Jerusalem and its ultimate consequence, when God abandons His temple in judgment, leaving it to be destroyed by the Babylonians. In chapters 40 – 46, Ezekiel sees a new temple with renewed worship within it. God returns to His temple. Once again, God will be with His people.

**6.** How is Ezekiel's vision of a new temple fulfilled? See John 1 v 14 and 2 v 18-22.

The temple of Ezekiel's vision was never built. When the people returned from exile, under the leadership of Ezra, they built a new temple. But it was nothing like the old one that Solomon had built, nor was it like Ezekiel's vision. Ezekiel's vision points to something better. The temple was only a symbol of God's presence with His people. The reality is Jesus. Jesus is "Immanuel"—"God with us".

## ⊟ **apply**

**7.** Ezekiel's vision of the new temple was to lead to new behaviour, by reminding the people of their sin (v 10) and of God's mercy (v 9) . This is even more true of the cross, where we see most clearly the extent of our sin and of the amazing mercy of God. When we understand the true significance of the cross, what behaviour should this lead to? Discuss specific areas.

- How can Christians help one another to maintain this kind of "cross-shaped" life?

- What happens when Christians start to forget about the cross?

## ⊡ explore more

**Read Mark 15 v 29-38.** In verse 29, those who pass by mock Jesus' claim to be the true temple. How do these verses show the similarities, and also the difference, between the temple built by Solomon, and Jesus?

| Solomon's temple | Jesus |
|---|---|
| abandoned by God | v 34 |
| destroyed by God's judgment | v 37 |
| keeping people from God (see Ezekiel 42 v 20) | v 38 |

# ⊕ investigate

> **Read Ezekiel 47 v 1-12**

**8.** Where does this river flow from?

God will not only cleanse the land, he will purify a third of the people.
These are the people who have remained faithful to God.

**9.** What effect does the river have?

**10.** Compare these verses with Revelation 22 v 1-3. What are the similarities?
And the differences?

Ezekiel 47 v 13 – 48 v 35 describes how the land is to be distributed
among the people of Israel. These instructions may seem dull to us, but to
the Israelites land meant everything. Land was their livelihood and their
identity. It was the assurance that they belonged. Ezekiel ends by revealing
the name of the city: 'THE LORD IS THERE' (48 v 35).

**11.** **Read Ephesians 1 v 13-14 and 1 Peter 1 v 3-5.** How can we know that
we have a share in God's new world?

Ezekiel has demolished our false hopes. There can be no hope when
God is against us. But in Jesus, God is for us. Ezekiel shows that there is
hope in God and His promises. And Ezekiel shows us what God
promises—a new people in a new world enjoying the presence of God.

## ⇥ apply

**12.** How should this hope affect the way we live now? See 1 Peter 3 v 8-15.

• How can Christians help one another to maintain this kind of hope-filled life?

• What happens when Christians start to doubt the hope of the new heaven and earth?

## ⊡ getting personal

What impression of your future would someone pick up from watching the way in which you live out your Christian faith? Would that impression be anything like Ezekiel's vision for God's people?

## ⬆ pray

Use Ezekiel chapters 40 – 48 as a basis for your prayer time. Don't forget to include points for thanksgiving as well as requests.

**Thank God...**

**Ask God...**

# The God of Glory
## Ezekiel
## LEADER'S GUIDE

# Leader's Guide

## Introduction

Leading a Bible study can be a bit like herding cats—everyone has a different idea of what the passage could be about, and a different line of enquiry that they want to pursue. But a good group leader is more than someone who just referees this kind of discussion. You will want to:

- **correctly understand** and handle the Bible passage. But also...

- **encourage and train** the people in your group to do this for themselves. Don't fall into the trap of spoon-feeding people by simply passing on the information in the Leader's Guide. Then...

- make sure that no Bible study is finished without everyone **knowing how the passage is relevant for them.** What changes do you all need to make in the light of the things you have been learning? And finally...

- encourage the group to turn all that has been learned and discussed into **prayer**.

Your Bible-study group is unique, and you are likely to know better than anyone the capabilities, backgrounds and circumstances of the people you are leading. That's why we've designed these guides with a number of optional features. If they're a quiet bunch, you might want to spend longer on **talkabout**. If your time is limited, you can choose to skip **explore more**, or get people to look at these questions at home. Can't get enough of Bible study? Well, some studies have optional extra homework projects. As leader, you can adapt and select the material to the needs of your particular group.

## So what's in the Leader's Guide?

The main thing that this Leader's Guide will help you to do is to understand the major teaching points in the passage you are studying, and how to apply them. As well as guidance on the questions, the Leader's Guide for each session contains the following important sections:

## THE BIG IDEA

One key sentence will give you the main point of the session. This is what you should be aiming to have fixed in people's minds as they leave the Bible study. And it's the point you need to head back towards when the discussion goes off at a tangent.

## SUMMARY

An overview of the passage, including plenty of useful historical background information.

## OPTIONAL EXTRA

Usually this is an introductory activity that ties in with the main theme of the Bible study, and is designed to "break the ice" at the beginning of a session. Or it may be a "homework project" that people can tackle during the week.

*So let's take a look at the various different features of a Good Book Guide.*

⊕ **talkabout:** each session kicks off with a discussion question, based on the group's opinions or experiences. It's designed to get people talking and thinking in a general way about the main subject of the Bible study.

⬇ **investigate:** the first thing that you and your group need to know is what the Bible passage is about, which is the purpose of these questions. But watch out—people may come up with answers based on their experiences or teaching they have heard in the past, without referring to the passage at all. It's amazing how often we can get through a Bible study without actually looking at the Bible! And if you're stuck for an answer, the Leader's Guide contains guidance on questions. These are the answers to which you need to direct your group. This information isn't meant to be read out to people—ideally, you want them to discover these answers from the Bible for themselves. Sometimes optional follow-up questions (see ⌄ in guidance on questions) are included, to help you help your group get to the answer.

⊡ **explore more:** these questions generally point people to other relevant parts of the Bible. They are useful for helping your group to see how the passage fits into the "big picture" of the whole Bible. These sections are **OPTIONAL**—only use them if you have time. Remember—it's better to finish in good time having really grasped one big thing from the passage, than to try and cram everything in.

⊟ **apply:** we want to encourage you to spend more time working at application—too often, it is simply tacked on at the end. In the **Good Book Guides**, apply sections are mixed in with the investigate sections of the study. We hope that people will realise that application is not just an optional extra, but rather, the whole purpose of studying the Bible. We do Bible study so that our lives can be changed by what we hear from God's word. If you skip the application, the Bible study hasn't achieved its purpose.

These questions draw out practical lessons that we can all learn from the Bible passage. You can review what has been learned so far, and think about practical differences that this should make in our churches and our lives. The group gets the opportunity to talk about what they personally have learned.

⊟ **getting personal** can be done at home, or you could allocate a few moments of quiet reflection for each person to think about specific changes that they need to make and pray through in their own lives.

Why not have a time for reporting back at the beginning of the following session, so that everyone can be encouraged and challenged by one another to make application a priority?

⬆ **pray:** In Acts 4 v 25-30 the first Christians quoted Psalm 2 as they prayed in response to the persecution of the apostles by the Jewish religious leaders. Today however, it's not as common for Christians to base prayers on the truths of God's word as it once was. As a result, our prayers tend to be weak, superficial and self-centred rather than bold, visionary and God-centred.

The prayer section is based on what has been learned from the Bible passage. How different our prayer times would be if we were genuinely responding to what God has said to us through His word.

## Ezekiel 1 – 3
# THE GOD OF GLORY

### THE BIG IDEA
God is at the centre of history, and should be at the centre of our lives.

### SUMMARY
The last remaining part of the nation of Israel (the southern kingdom of Judah) has been defeated by the Babylonians, the current regional superpower. The ruling elite—the king, the royal court, the religious leaders, the promising young men (including Daniel)—have all been taken into exile in Babylon. A puppet regime has been installed in Jerusalem. Ezekiel was among the exiles who were taken into Babylon. During Ezekiel's ministry, the Israelites who remained in Palestine unsuccessfully rebelled against Babylon (see 2 Kings 24 – 25). Jerusalem and the temple were destroyed (Ezekiel 33).

It must have seemed to the exiles that God had abandoned them, or that He was weaker than the Babylonian gods. So the book of Ezekiel opens with a magnificent vision of God. Ezekiel sees the power and splendour of God. God is seated on a throne that moves, for His rule is not confined to one place. In addition, Ezekiel sees this vision in Babylon. It highlights God's power over all nations.

Ezekiel refers to this opening vision a number of times in his ministry. The repeated theme of the book is: "Then they will know that I am the Lord". God is at the centre of Ezekiel's view of the world.

But Ezekiel is also told that the people will reject his message because they are a rebellious people. People, then and now, do not reject God's word because it is hard to understand, but because they do not want to obey God.

### OPTIONAL EXTRA
Divide your group into pairs and give them a few minutes to come up with some endings to the phrase "If I were God…" These may be based on things that people have been heard to say, or on songs such as: "If I ruled the world", or perhaps people in the group have themselves been tempted to make a statement like this. Discuss what this reveals about humanity's view of both God and ourselves.
The central idea of this session, that the universe is God-centred, should blow this kind of thinking away.

### GUIDANCE ON QUESTIONS
**2.** You could turn to Psalm 137 to find out how the exiles felt.

**3.** The exiles might have thought that God was weaker than the Babylonian gods, or that He had abandoned them.

**4.** See 1 v 3. Ezekiel sees this vision of God in **enemy territory**. God is not confined to the land of Israel. He rules over all nations.

**5.** Flashing lightning, brilliant light, glowing metal, supernatural creatures, wonderful jewels—all show that God is great, holy and glorious.

**6.**

- **What can a throne with wheels do?**
- **What does this tell us about God?**
- **What do we learn about the wheels?**
- **What does this tell us?**

God is not just the God of the physical land of Israel. The movement of the creatures and the wheels symbolises God's rule over all the earth—even in Babylon. And the rim of eyes in verse 18 reminds us that God sees the plight of His people.

**7.** See verse 28. An encounter with the living God leaves you flat on your face! See also 3 v 15.

**8. APPLY: Prayers:** Often directed towards our needs and goals instead of God's mercy and glory (see optional extra below).
**Evangelism:** Can communicate how God meets people's desires, without also calling on people to submit to God and glorify His name. The goal of mission is God's glory.
**Meetings:** May tend to focus on "me and my emotions", rather than on who God is and what He has done.
- The root of all sin is the illicit desire to be like God (Genesis 3 v 4-6), so it follows that sinful human nature will always tend towards putting humans at the centre of the universe, rather than God. But Romans 8 v 12-14 tells us that Christians have an obligation, and

an ability through God's Spirit, not to live according to our sinful natures, but to put this kind of tendency to death.
- Get the group to discuss how human-centred Christianity will affect things such as our faith in God, our response to God when our desires are not met, our understanding of God when things get tough, the quality of Christian commitment and service in our churches, the church's ability to withstand cultural pressure or persecution, our attitude to God's word etc.

## OPTIONAL EXTRA
To follow up question 8, look at some Bible prayers. Identify the requests made in Bible prayers and the reasons used. Compare them with our typical prayers. You could use Numbers 14 v 13-19; Isaiah 37 v 15-20; Daniel 9 v 4-19; Matthew 6 v 9-13; Philippians 1 v 9-11; 2 Thessalonians 1 v 11-12.

### EXPLORE MORE
God made humanity in His likeness. We were designed to be like God. God appears human because He is what we were meant to be like. But this vision also points forward to the time when God will become a man in the person of Jesus. The apostle John uses the language of Ezekiel to describe the risen Christ in Revelation 1. We may not see a vision of God's glory as Ezekiel did. But we have seen God's glory revealed even more fully in the life, death and resurrection of His Son, Jesus.

**9.** It is not the most motivational call to evangelism! Ezekiel is told to speak to people who will not listen. Ezekiel is not yet told what his message will be—simply that it is God's word (2 v 4; 3 v 11).

**10.** Look at 3 v 6. People do not reject God's Word because they cannot understand what is said—it is not obscure or difficult. The problem is that they will not accept God's word. It is sometimes said that modern science makes it impossible to believe Christianity. But the problem is not that the message is unbelieveable, but that people will not submit to God's word. It is a problem of the heart, not of the head.

### EXPLORE MORE

These references reinforce the answer to question 9. The fool of Psalm 14 is not ignorant or stupid. He is morally corrupt. He says "there is no God" because he will not obey God. In Romans 1 Paul says the truth about God is plain, but people have suppressed the truth. Our hearts have become darkened because we have rejected God's lordship over our lives.

**11.** God's word will sustain Ezekiel and keep him from sharing the rebellion of the people (2 v 8 – 3 v 3). God will strengthen him and be with him so there is no need to be afraid (3 v 8-13). God also reminds Ezekiel of His glory (3 v 22-23) and enables him to speak (3 v 24-27). You may want to draw out the parallels with your own experience.

**12. APPLY:** A faithful life may persuade more readily than a clever argument because it challenges people's rebellion and rebellion is the real problem behind unbelief.

**13. APPLY: 1 Corinthians 2 v 1-5:** Successful evangelism does not depend on eloquence or human wisdom ie: our powers of persuasion or our ability to reason. It does depend on a demonstration of the Spirit's power, which is shown as Christians, like Paul, speak the message with weakness and fear—quite the opposite characteristics that most of us would look for in an effective evangelist!

- **2 Corinthians 4 v 1-6:** We proclaim Christ crucified as Lord, setting forth the truth plainly. At the same time, we pray that God will open blind eyes to see the light of the knowledge of the glory of God in the face of Christ.

**14. APPLY:** The problems we face are not unique to our generation. Ezekiel also had to minister to hard hearts. But God has preserved His people and His gospel. Above all, these chapters remind us of God's glory and His rule over all nations.

# Ezekiel 4 – 24
# THE GOD OF JUDGMENT

## THE BIG IDEA
God is against humanity because of our rebellion, and our only hope is in God Himself.

## SUMMARY
Ezekiel chapters 4 – 24 are addressed to Israel. God had placed Israel among the nations as a light to those nations. But Israel had rebelled against God's lordship and dishonoured His name. And so God is now against His people. He will bring judgment on them through Babylon. In this way He will demonstrate that He is Lord and re-establish the honour of His name.

## OPTIONAL EXTRA
Begin by using a contemporary song, film clip, painting or extract from literature that expresses our culture's false hopes or sense of hopelessness.

## GUIDANCE ON QUESTIONS
**1.** Answers can include both hopes for human progress and hopes for life after death.

**2.** See 5 v 12. What happens to Ezekiel's hair will be what happens to the people of Israel. A third will die from plague, a third by the sword and a third will be scattered. But a faithful few will be saved, represented by the strands of hair tucked away in Ezekiel's clothing (5 v 3).

**3.** See 5 v 5. According to Deuteronomy 4 v 5-8, God's people were meant to show the nations that the rule of God brought freedom and life as they lived under His law.

**4.** See 5 v 6-7. God's people have not even lived up to the standards of the nations, let alone God's good law.

**5. APPLY:** The group can discuss specific opportunities of contact with non-Christians in their community and through personal circumstances.
- **Titus 2 v 1-10** shows that it is the practical outworking of Christian standards in everyday life (rather than, say, attendance at Christian meetings, or subscribing to Christian creeds) which provides the powerful witness to the message of the gospel that Christians are called to give.
- Get people to come up with examples eg: Matthew 5 v 38-47, 1 Peter 2 v 18-23.
- "No-one will malign the word of God" (Titus 2 v 5); people will have nothing bad to say about Christians (v 8); the teaching of God our Saviour will be made attractive (v10).

**6.** The people doubted God's warnings of judgment would ever happen, or that they would happen soon. They reinforced these doubts or false hopes by listening to false prophets, who would tell them what they wanted to hear.

The false prophets were saying there would be peace, but there would be no peace (13 v 10).

**7.** Ezekiel systematically dismantled the people's false hopes. God's warnings of judgment would come to pass (12 v 25)—and soon (12 v 28). The 'storm' of God's judgment would come (13 v 11). The people's false hopes were like whitewash that would be swept away in the rain (13 v 12).

**EXPLORE MORE**
The people complain that they are being judged for the sins of their ancestors. It was true that Israel was defeated by Babylon because successive generations had rebelled against God. But God says that each person is judged according to what they have done—no one is judged for the sins of others. If individuals are judged each according to their own actions, there is no hope for any of us. Our only hope is to turn to God in repentance and receive forgiveness from Him. The ultimate evidence that God takes "no pleasure in the death of the wicked" is the cross. God sent His Son to die in our place, so that we can receive life through Jesus.

**8.** The delight of Ezekiel's eyes was his wife; the delight of the people of Israel was the temple (v 21). There seems to be nothing wrong with Ezekiel's delight in his wife, but God's judgment in destroying the temple shows that it was clearly wrong for the people to delight in the temple—it had become a substitute for delighting in the Lord. The parallel with Ezekiel's delight in his wife highlights the fervency, not the legitimacy, of the people's devotion to the temple.

**9.** God would desecrate His own sanctuary (v 21).
• This is shocking because the temple was planned and set up by God Himself as the way by which His people could meet with Him. Even things provided by God to help His people must not be allowed to take His place in our hearts as the supreme object of our love and trust.

**10.** God did this to reduce the people to despair (v23); the final outcome would be "You will know that I am the Sovereign LORD"— a refrain that runs throughout Ezekiel's message, repeated in one form or another more than 60 times. The people had rejected the lordship of God. They had thrown His lordship into question. But God would demonstrate that He is the Lord by judging their rebellion. Israel should have been a light to the nations, but instead the nations had profaned His name. And so God would demonstrate the honour of His name through their judgment.

**11. APPLY:** People find false hope in **religion** (we can make ourselves right with God); in **consumerism** (we can find fulfilment and identity through consumer goods); in **humanism** (human beings can solve their problems by themselves). Examples of false teaching in **churches** include those who give false hope beyond death, by denying God's judgment in the name of His love; or those who give false hope in this life by promising health and wealth in the name of Jesus.
• **2 Timothy 4 v 1-5:** They say what people want to hear; they turn people away from the truth; they get caught up with myths.
• See 2 Timothy 4 verses 2 and 5.

**12. APPLY:** Encourage the group to discuss how their understanding of God has changed.

- God will not allow anything to take His place in our hearts.
- In 2 Corinthians 11 v 2-4 Paul reflects God's jealousy for the affection of His people in his desire for Christians to stay single-heartedly devoted to Jesus and to reject all other "gospels".
- Although it's not mentioned in the passages from Ezekiel investigated in this session, the rest of the Bible (eg: 1 Timothy 6 v 17) makes clear that the only hope for humans is hope in God. This is the reason why Ezekiel demolishes the false hopes of the people, and why God destroys the false object of their pride and delight. Only when people are reduced to despair by the loss of these things will they turn to God. It is the gospel of Jesus that remedies this human despair (see Isaiah 61 v 1-3 and Luke 4 v 17-21).

## PRAY

These are some of the points that may come out of the passage to pray and praise God for:

**Thank God…**

- that He doesn't put up with sin and rebellion forever—evil will be ended!
- that He will demolish people's false hopes and even cause despair, so that they might find true hope in His name.
- that He takes no pleasure in the death of anyone and has sent Jesus, through whom we can all repent and live.

**Ask God…**

- to help you to be a light to those around you, and make the teaching about God our Saviour attractive.
- for people you know to give up their false hopes and look instead to God.
- to help you and your church recognise and resist any false prophets that can take you away from delighting in the Lord.

# 3 Ezekiel 25 – 32
# THE GOD OF THE NATIONS

## THE BIG IDEA
God is the God of all people and He is against us because of our rebellion.

## SUMMARY
In chapters 4 – 24, Ezekiel addressed the nation of Israel. He had two repeated phrases: "Then you will know that I am the Lord" and "I am against you". In chapters 25 – 32, Ezekiel addresses the nations around Israel. And his message to them is the same. The same two phrases are repeated. The nations too will know that God is the Lord. Israel's God is the God of all humanity. And God is against the nations because of their rebellion. Israel's fate will be the fate of all humanity.

Israel looked to the economic might of Tyre and the military might of Egypt, but Ezekiel shows us that these are false hopes when God is against you.

## OPTIONAL EXTRA
Plot the countries that Ezekiel talks about on a map. You will see that Ezekiel moves anti-clockwise around Israel.

Ask different members of the group to come with prayer information on particular missionaries or countries. Somebody could draw attention to information from a recent missionary prayer letter, while someone else could highlight the needs of a country with which they have contact in some way.

## GUIDANCE ON QUESTIONS
**1.** Discussion may highlight people's reluctance to proclaim one God for all people in a society that preaches that "all religions lead to God".

**2.** The nations rejoiced in Israel's judgment and took advantage of it to express their malice.

**3.** Tyre used her trading power to exploit others (28 v 16, 18). And her success made her proud (v 17).

### EXPLORE MORE
In Revelation Babylon represents Rome— the latest superpower to oppose God and His people. In Ezekiel 26 v 15-18 and Revelation 18 v 9-10, we read that the kings of the earth lament the fall of Tyre and Rome, while Ezekiel 27 v 25-36 and Revelation 18 v 14-19 describe the mourning of the merchants and seafarers. Just as Tyre used her trading power to exploit others, and just as she became proud (Ezekiel 28 v 16-18), so Rome has exploited others (Revelation 18 v 3) and has become proud (Revelation 18 v 7). John tells his readers to "come out of her" (Revelation 18 v 4). This could lead to a discussion of what it might mean to disassociate (to "come out") from the exploitation and pride of trade today.

**4.** See 29 v 6-7 and 16. Israel looked to Egypt for military security and, although not directly mentioned here, to Tyre for economic security. But they should have looked to God. These chapters are designed to be overheard by God's people. They are a reminder that God is Lord of the nations and that the ultimate confidence of His people should be in Him.

**5. APPLY:** Substitutes for trust in God can include:
**For personal security**—a healthy savings account, loads of possessions, living near your family, sticking to a large prosperous church. (Matthew 6 v 19-21 warns against storing up treasures on earth.)
**For social problems and threats to our way of life**—political influence, economic might, professional PR and a respectable public profile, media access, allegiance with society's "movers and shakers" (Isaiah 31 v 1 warns against trusting in those things that provide worldly power.)
**For solutions to the weakness of the church**—compromising the message to make it more attractive; substituting, for the teaching of God's word, big spectacular events offering experiences; using celebrities or academics to gain credence in popular culture or academic circles. (1 Corinthians 1 v 20-25 warns against relying on worldly wisdom in gospel ministry.)
• Israel were damaged by their reliance on Egypt. Similarly, the church will be damaged by relying on these substitutes for God.

**6.** "I am against you". There is no need to take a long time over questions 6-9, once people have seen the parallel between Ezekiel's message to Israel and his message to the nations.

**7.** It is the same message: "I am against you". See also 28 v 22; 29 v 3, 10; 30 v 22.

**8.** "Then you will know that I am the Lord." See also 7 v 4, 27.

**9.** It is the same message: "Then you will know that I am the Lord". See also 26 v 6; 28 v 22, 23, 24, 26; 29 v 6, 9, 16, 21; 30 v 8, 19, 25, 26;  32 v 15.

**10.** Some of the nations delighted in Israel's downfall (25 v 6). But just as God is against Israel, so He is against the nations because of their rebellion. Israel's fate will be their fate. Point out that this includes us as we read these accounts.
**11.** Some of the nations misunderstood Israel's downfall (25 v 8). They thought it meant that Israel's God was no better than their gods. But God says the nations will know that He is the Lord. Israel's God is the God of all nations.

**12. APPLY:** They don't listen to God because they don't believe that He is speaking specifically to them, and so they end up not believing in Him at all.
• Somebody might accept the validity of Israel's religious experience, but might want to say that other religions are equally valid. These chapters claim that the God of the Bible is the God of all nations. And one day all humanity will know that He is the Lord.
• **Our prayers:** We should be praying for all nations and cultures;
**Our evangelism:** Everyone that hears our message should know that the God of the Bible is their God; **Our meetings:** Church should never be a national club but welcoming and relevant to those of all nations; **Our friendships:** We should be open to cross-cultural friendships, including those of other faiths, in the hope that we can also bring the Word of God to our international friends; **Our involvement in international mission**: It's not optional!

## Ezekiel 33 – 36
# THE GOD OF HOPE

## THE BIG IDEA
We need more than a fresh start: we need God to rescue us, cleanse us and give us new hearts with His Spirit within us.

## SUMMARY
In chapters 4 – 24 Ezekiel destroys all the false hopes of Israel. Judgment is coming. In 24 v 25-27 we learn that Ezekiel will have nothing more to say until judgment has come—until a fugitive comes, bringing the news that Jerusalem has fallen. In 33 v 21 that fugitive turns up. It is the pivotal point in the book. Whereas chapters 1 – 32 have been about false hopes, chapters 34 – 48 are about finding true hope. We find true hope in God and in His promises. God Himself will rescue us, cleanse us and give us a new heart with His Spirit within us. Ezekiel's message of judgment in chapters 4 – 32 was introduced with a warning to Ezekiel to be a watchman (see 3 v 16-21). His message of hope is introduced in the same way (see 33 v 1-9). We have a responsibility to warn of God's judgment and point to the hope of the gospel.

## OPTIONAL EXTRA
Apparently lifeguards and maritime rescuers are trained to avoid someone who is thrashing about in the water trying to swim. Instead, they should wait nearby until the person is completely exhausted and has given up, before going to their aid. Other situations where people cannot be helped, because of false hopes or false confidence in themselves, might include addiction or serious illness, where someone refuses to go to rehab or the doctor. Ask a couple of people to role-play one or more of these situations. As they do so, discuss both why the victim can't be helped and what needs to happen.

## GUIDANCE ON QUESTIONS
**1.** Examples might include starting out on the wrong foot with someone, or making a bad impression on the first day at work or school. You could also ask whether anyone has had the opportunity to make a fresh start. Did it go better the second time around? Ezekiel promises that God will give His people a fresh start, but in fact, it will be so much more than a fresh start.

**2.** The people believe that if Abraham was able to possess the land, even though he was only one person, then certainly those of the nation who are left could also possess the land again. They think that by their military might ("your sword" in 33 v 26) they can recapture the land.

- **How was Abraham able to possess the land?** (see Genesis 15 v 7). Abraham did not possess the land because of his military might, but because God promised it to him.
- **Why is that no longer possible for Israel?** Look back at 5 v 8. But now God is against His people.

## EXPLORE MORE

The people liked listening to Ezekiel because he was an interesting eccentric. Listening to him was an amusing pastime. But they did not take his message seriously, nor did they put it into practice. It is important for talks and Bible studies to engage the hearers, but even more important that they are faithful to God's word. What makes a good talk or Bible study is whether people put God's word into practice (see v 31-32 and James 1 v 22-25).

**3.** God describes the leaders of Israel as shepherds and He describes the people as His flock. The leaders of Israel have neglected the flock. They have been concerned only with their own interests.

**4.** God Himself will shepherd His people. Ask people to identify all the times God says "I will". What will God do in each case?

**5.** Or "Through whom will God shepherd His people?" God will send a new King David to care for His people. David was the shepherd who became Israel's greatest king.

## EXPLORE MORE

Verse 11 emphasises that God Himself will shepherd His people, while in verse 23, He says the new "King David" will shepherd them. Will God Himself rescue His sheep or will God's king do it? John 10 shows that it is Jesus who fulfils this promise, and the answer to this apparent tension is that Jesus is both God and God's Shepherd-King. (eg: Jesus is both the Son of God and the Son of David— Romans 1 v 4). Jesus lays down His life for His sheep (unlike all other so-called shepherds) and He speaks to them. He is so powerful that nothing and no one can remove His sheep from His care.

**6. APPLY:** We should respond to Jesus our Shepherd-King with trust and confidence. He has the authority of God's chosen King and uses that authority to care for His people. **Psalm 23:** Words that would summarise our relationship with the Shepherd-King could include dependence, trust, follow, safety, blessed, gratitude etc.

- Draw attention to the contrast between the shepherds of Ezekiel 34 v 1-10, and the example of Jesus, used by Peter to teach church leaders (see optional extra below).

- Our natural tendency is to fear things that threaten us rather than confidently trust the One who can and will protect and provide for us. Encourage people to discuss their fears and how confidence in Jesus might help them overcome those fears.

## OPTIONAL EXTRA

Jesus is the "great Shepherd of the sheep" (Hebrews 13 v 20-21). Use the following table to answer question 7.

| The bad shepherds of Israel | The great Shepherd of the sheep |
|---|---|
| no compassion for the sheep | see Matthew 9 v 36 |
| do not bring back the strays | see Luke 15 v 3-7 |
| act out of self-interest | see John 10 v 11-16 |

**7.** Key themes mentioned in these verses are: safety (v 25, 28); prosperity (v 26-27); rescue from slavery (v 27); renown among the nations (v 29); intimacy with God (v 30-31).

## EXPLORE MORE

Hebrews 11 v 11-16 and 39-40 tell us that God's promise of a land to Abraham and his descendants was understood, by those who had true faith, to have a far greater fulfilment than the physical land of Israel. The fulfilment would be a heavenly one that God's people did not receive during their lives on earth. Romans 8 v 19-21 and Revelation 21 v 1 show us that God will restore the whole of creation—this is the "better heavenly country". The promise of a land becomes the promise that God's people will inherit the whole earth, as indicated by Matthew 5 v 5.

**8.** God will save His people for the sake of His holy name—so that He will be glorified (v 21-23). Throughout the book, Ezekiel's refrain has been: "Then they will know that I am the LORD".

**9.**

• **What would the nations think of God when they saw Israel's sin?**

God's people had brought God's name into disrepute. They were supposed to live under God's rule according to His law in such a way that the nations would recognise the goodness of God's rule. But God's people did not live righteously. They gave the nations a wrong picture of God. So God judged His people to demonstrate that He was not like them. He proved His holiness and goodness by judging their injustice and evil·

**10.**

• **What would the nations think of God when they saw Israel defeated and exiled?**

God's name was honoured by the judgment of Israel. But now the nations would say: "Israel's God cannot care for His people or keep His promise". And so God would save His people for the sake of His holy name. He would protect His reputation by proving that He could keep His promise and rescue His people.

**11.** As in Ezekiel's day, God glorifies His name through judgment and salvation. God is glorified as He displays His holiness and justice in His judgment on sinners. And God is glorified as He displays His holiness, justice, love and mercy by saving sinners through the cross.

**12.** If God simply gave us a fresh start, then we would make a mess of our lives all over again. But God promises to cleanse His people. And He promises to give us a new heart with His Spirit within us. God not only gives us a fresh start, He forgives our sins and gives us the power to live for Him.

**13. APPLY:** Ezekiel 36 v 25 talks about cleansing from impurity—the removal of the desire to sin. Verse 27 talks about God's Spirit moving us to follow His laws— this involves listening to God's word and putting it into practice. These are two key changes that we should expect to see in anyone who claims to be a Christian. This question is a chance to explore in practice what it means for God to give us new hearts with His Spirit within us.
**1 John 1 v 8-9:** Clearly Christians still sin, but we confess our sins and seek forgiveness.
**John 10 v 27:** True Christians always respond to God's Word with a hunger to learn more and a desire to do it.
• We should be sceptical of the claims of those who call themselves Christians, but show no evidence of these changes.

# 5 Ezekiel 37 – 39
# THE GOD OF LIFE

## THE BIG IDEA
We can have hope because God provides life, unity and protection to His people.

## SUMMARY
In 37 v 1-14 Ezekiel sees a valley of dry, lifeless bones. They represent the people of God who are without hope.

But, through His word and by his Spirit, God gives them new life and new hope. This vision does not, in the first place, speak about individual life after death. It speaks of hope beyond judgment. We can still know God (which is what true life consists of) despite our sin, through the life-giving work of God's Spirit, through His word. This life-giving work is called "regeneration".

When King Rehoboam, the son of King Solomon, became king of Israel, he ruled over the people harshly and provoked a revolution. The nation split into two. But in 37 v 15-28 Ezekiel promises that God will gather His scattered people and reunite them under a new King David. As the Bible unfolds, it becomes clear that God's ultimate plan is to gather people from many nations (see 38 v 8) under the kingship of Jesus. Through the gospel, people from all nations are reconciled to God and to each other.

In chapters 38 – 39 Ezekiel speaks of Gog and Magog. They are names from Israel's ancient history (see Genesis 10 v 1-3). Ezekiel uses them symbolically to represent all those throughout history who have opposed God and His people. God promises to protect His people and bring glory to His name by defeating His enemies.

## OPTIONAL EXTRA
You could begin by showing an extract from a film in which everything seems hopeless. You could, for example, show the climax of Lord of the Rings: The Two Towers. You could then also note the similarities with the attack of the armies of Magog when you discuss question 8.

## GUIDANCE ON QUESTIONS
**2.** See verse 11. The dry bones represent the whole house of Israel. This vision does not, in the first place, speak about individual life after death. It speaks of hope beyond judgment. It shows how we can still know God (which is what true life consists of) despite our sin.

**3.** God brings new life through His word and His Spirit working together.

**4. APPLY:** Answers could include the following: only God can give life, spiritual or physical; unsaved people are dead in their sins and there is nothing that they, or we, can do to help them apart from bringing them the gospel; God's life-giving Spirit works when Ezekiel is faithful (even though the task seems ludicrous) and obeys God by preaching His word. These lessons should affect our ministry in the following ways: our priority must be preaching the word, and praying for God's Spirit to use the word to open people's hearts; we must be faithful in doing this even though this way of doing things is derided by outsiders; we should renounce manipulation or deception as a means of persuasion.

- Some churches emphasise the centrality of God's word, while others emphasise the importance of the work of God's Spirit. So sometimes people call for balance, as if we can pick and choose from one or the other. But if God's word and Spirit work together, we cannot have one without the other. God works by His Spirit through His word. Think what this might mean for your group and your church.
- Give the group an opportunity to discuss how this striking story has impacted them.

**5.** God is going to unite His people once again. He is going to reconcile them to one another. Both the northern and southern kingdoms had been scattered to the nations, but it would seem from these verses that God was planning to gather them together again (v 21). Historically however, the northern kingdom of Israel was never again re-united with the southern kingdom of Judah. The fulfilment of this promise is found elsewhere (see question 7 below).

**6.** King David was the shepherd who became Israel's greatest King. The prophets describe God's coming King as a new King David. He will be even greater than Israel's greatest king. The people will live under God's reign, expressed in His law. They will live in the land that God promised to them. They will live in peace forever. God Himself will be with them. Not all this was fulfilled in the history of the nation of Israel. But the New Testament shows that Jesus is God's promised King. We will live under His reign of peace forever in the new creation and God will be with us.

**EXPLORE MORE**
2 Corinthians 6 v 16 tells us that Christians are the temple of God—He lives among Christians in this world. Revelation 21 v 3 tells us that in the new heaven and earth God will live among His forgiven people.

**7.** God's plan was not to politically unite the tribes of Israel, but to unite Jew and Gentile in Christ. God will gather people from many nations (see 38 v 8). Through the gospel, people from all nations are reconciled to God and to each other. God's wisdom is made known in spiritual realms through the unity of the church (Ephesians 3 v 10). So in the church, we are to do all we can to maintain this unity (Ephesians 4 v 1-3). Encourage people to explore together the practical implications of this in your situation.

**8.** King Gog, from the land of Magog, will come with his army against the restored people of God. The armies of Magog will attack God's peaceful people in order to plunder and destroy them.

**9.** The hope mentioned in chapter 38 is that God crushes the enemies of His people. So God will defend His people and give them victory, showing His supreme greatness and complete holiness in the sight of many nations.
The hope in chapter 39 v 21-29 is that

God will restore His people and fulfil His promises to them.

**10.** God's great purpose is to establish the holiness and glory of His name (see 38 v 16 and 23 and also 36 v 23). He does this by allowing His enemies to come against His people, using all the might that they can muster, before executing judgment on them at the very moment when their victory seems assured. God shows Himself holy to the nations, both by bringing His enemies in judgment against His people (38 v 16) and by destroying those enemies (38 v 22-23).

**11. APPLY:** In many parts of the world the church faces persecution including violence and imprisonment. Even where there is no threat of violence, the church faces pressures from society to conform to its ways rather than to God's ways. You could discuss the different ways people in the group feel this pressure.
• The fact that God does not always

intervene now to rescue His people from persecution does not mean we should doubt His final victory. These passages from Ezekiel show us that God's reason for delay is to better show the nations His holiness and greatness.
• Ezekiel 39 v 26 tells us that Israel became unfaithful to God when they lived in safety. Troubles make us turn to God in repentance and dependence on Him.
• We can be helped to stand firm in the face of persecution if we understand and trust God's purposes in allowing these situations, and if we are confident of God's final victory over His enemies. What matters is that God's name is glorified. And God's name is glorified when we are faithful to Him—especially in the face of opposition.

## OPTIONAL EXTRA
Ask someone within the group to bring information for prayer on the persecuted church around the world.

# 6

## Ezekiel 40 – 48
# THE GOD OF THE FUTURE

### THE BIG IDEA
God promises a new world in which His people will enjoy His presence.

### SUMMARY
The book of Ezekiel ends with a vision of a new temple in a new Jerusalem. In chapters 8 – 10, Ezekiel saw God's glory leave the temple. God abandoned His temple in judgment on the corrupt worship that was taking place within it. And in judgment, the temple was destroyed. Now Ezekiel sees a new temple with renewed worship. And he sees God's glory return to the temple. God is once again among His people. From the new temple flows a river that brings life. By the river are trees that provide food and give healing to God's people. It is a picture of Eden restored. And the name of the city is "The LORD is There". Ezekiel describes the distribution of the land to God's new people. This was to be their assurance of belonging. The temple of Ezekiel's vision was never built. When the people returned from exile, under the leadership of Ezra, they built a new temple, but it was not built to Ezekiel's design. Ezekiel's vision points to Jesus (John 2 v 18-22). Jesus is "God with us". The apostle John uses the language of Ezekiel to describe the new Jerusalem (Revelation 22 v 1-3). Our inheritance is in heaven (1 Peter 1 v 3-5). We find assurance that we will share in God's new world when we receive the Holy Spirit and believe the gospel (Ephesians 1 v 13-14).

### OPTIONAL EXTRA
As a prelude to this session, which focuses on our hope in God's future, if anyone in your group has coaching experience, ask them to share how they motivate their team or athletes to be successful and get through the grind of training. Or discuss with your group what would help them succeed in an arduous but achievable fund-raising challenge (eg: a half-marathon, a 24-hour fast,) and conversely, what would make them want to quit.

### GUIDANCE ON QUESTIONS
**1.** People's image of heaven will probably reflect their personality. Some may imagine a country scene, others a vast praise meeting, others an endless football match.

**2.** Ezekiel's vision of the future reflects his training as a priest. He imagines a new temple in a new Jerusalem. Ezekiel's description of the new temple in chapters 40 – 46 can seem somewhat boring to us. But Ezekiel's "tour-guide" tells him to pay attention to all that he sees.

**3.** The Spirit of God lifts Ezekiel up and brings him to the temple. Ezekiel sees a vision of God's glory, like the vision he saw by the Kebar River in chapter 1. And he sees God's glory moving in the temple.

**4.** In chapter 10 the glory of God departed from the temple (10 v 18). But in chapter 43 the glory of God enters the temple and fills it (43 v 4-5).

**5.** The holy God is going to live among His people again, so they should get rid of anything unholy ( v 7, 9-10). They have seen His judgment against sin ( v 8). They have seen the beauty of God's new temple and they should not want to spoil it in anyway (v 11).

**6.** See John 1 v 14 and John 2 v 18-22. We see the glory of God in Jesus, and in Him, God's glory comes to His people. Jesus is the true temple. God is present with us through Jesus, and Jesus is the one through whom we can know God.

**7. APPLY:** You may want to ask this question of specific areas such as—our response when people let us down, the use of our money and time; our attitude to the marginalised in society. So, for example, when people let us down, we remember that we let God down big time and yet, He still loved us and gave His Son for us.
• In our preaching, praise and encouragement of one another, we continually need to return to the cross, as the foundation, motivation and example of all that we do as Christians. Don't think of it as just milk for spiritual babies, which you give up when you grow as Christians. True spiritual food is learning how to apply the lessons of the cross to every part of our lives.
• When Christians forget the cross, we fall into one of two errors: legalism, because we have forgotten God's grace

to sinners shown through the cross; or licence (living without any standards of Christian conduct), because we have forgotten God's refusal to compromise with sin, shown by His judgment of our sin on the cross.

| Solomon's temple | Jesus |
| --- | --- |
| abandoned by God | abandoned by God (Mark 15 v 34) |
| destroyed by God's judgment | killed because of God's judgment (Mark 15 v 37) |
| keeping people from God (see Ezekiel 42 v 20) | bringing people to God (Mark 15 v 38) |

**8.** The river flows from the altar in the temple—the place of sacrifice. For sinners to be forgiven and reconciled to God a sacrifice (of death) is needed that is sufficient to pay the penalty for our sin that God's justice demands. The sacrificial death of Jesus means that God can show mercy without compromising His holiness and justice. God can now bless His sinful people with life instead of punishing them with death.

**9.** The river brings life wherever it goes. It turns salt water into fresh water. It enables trees to bear fruit all year round, providing food and healing to God's people.

**10.** The apostle John uses the language of Ezekiel to describe the new heaven and earth. Both passages speak of a river that brings life. In Revelation, the trees are the tree of life (a reference to the garden of Eden) and they bring healing to all nations (not just Israel). And the river flows from the throne of God and the Lamb (Jesus). It is the sacrifice of the Lamb that brings life.

**11.** We know that we share in God's new world when, through the Spirit, we hear and believe the gospel (Ephesians 1 v 13). The Holy Spirit guarantees our inheritance (Ephesians 1 v 13-14). Our inheritance is kept for us by God (1 Peter 1 v 4), and we are kept for our inheritance (1 Peter 1 v 5).

**12. APPLY:** You could also use the following references to answer this question: Matthew 6 v 19-21; Colossians 3 v 1-4; Hebrews 11 v 13-16; 2 Peter 3 v 10-13 and 1 John 3 v 2-3.

- We need to talk about our hope and inheritance when we are together, reminding each other of what we have to look forward to when we are confronted by death, hardships, temptation or opposition.
- When we doubt or forget about our hope, we become focused on this world, distracted by stuff that seems important now, and discouraged by the difficulties of the Christian life. We can end up as unprofitable servants, wasting our time on things that won't last, while gospel ministry is neglected.

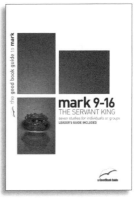

# thegoodbook
## COMPANY

At The Good Book Company, we are dedicated to helping Christians and local churches grow. We believe that God's growth process always starts with hearing clearly what he has said to us through his timeless word—the Bible.

Ever since we opened our doors in 1991, we have been striving to produce resources that honour God in the way the Bible is used. We have grown to become an international provider of user-friendly resources to the Christian community, with believers of all backgrounds and denominations using our Bible studies, books, evangelistic resources, DVD-based courses and training events.

We want to equip ordinary Christians to live for Christ day by day, and churches to grow in their knowledge of God, their love for one another, and the effectiveness of their outreach. Call us for a discussion of your needs or visit one of our local websites for more information on the resources and services we provide.

**UK & Europe: www.thegoodbook.co.uk**
**N America: www.thegoodbook.com**
**Australia: www.thegoodbook.com.au**
**New Zealand: www.thegoodbook.co.nz**

**UK & Europe: 0333 123 0880**
**N America: 866 244 2165**
**Australia: (02) 6100 4211**
**New Zealand (+64) 3 343 1990**

## Also part of the Good Book Guide series...

**In the beginning** 7 studies
(Genesis 1 – 4)

**Living in the real world**
(1 Peter) 5 studies

**God of glory**
(Ezekiel) 6 studies

**The coming King**
(Mark 1-8) 10 studies

**The servant King**
(Mark 9-16) 7 studies

**God's big plan for struggling Christians** (Zechariah) 6 studies

**Women of faith** 8 studies
**from the Old Testament**

**Introducing Jesus** 7 studies
(John)

**Living to please God** 7 studies
(1 Thessalonians)

**Experiencing God** 6 studies

**Soul songs** (Psalms) 6 studies

**Consider Jesus** (Hebrews) 8 studies

**A message from Jesus to the church today** (Revelation 2-3)
7 studies

*You can find more Good Book Guides from the series on your local website*